The Gold Shop of Ba-'Ali

THE GOLD SHOP OF BA-'ALI

poems by

Yahya Frederickson

LOST HORSE PRESS
Sandpoint, Idaho

ACKNOWLEDGMENTS

Thanks to the editors of the following journals for publishing poems in this collection, or earlier versions of them:

Clackamas Literary Review: "First Fast"
Crab Orchard Review: "Rite"
The Cream City Review: "Cattle from Ethiopia"
Cutthroat: "The Bus to Aden," "The Gold Shop of Ba-'Ali"
Flyway: "Praying beside a *Mujahed*"
Islamica: "Embrace," "The Gold Shop of Ba-'Ali" (reprint), "The Stone Polisher"
Al-Masar: "All-Night Teashop"; "Revolution Day"; "Crossing" (previously titled "*Bab al-Sabah* Market"); "*Qahwa al-Baidhani*," "*Duqq*," and "*Qishr*" appeared as "*Arabica*"
Quarter After Eight: "Secession"
Rag Mag: "Aden," "Balhaf," "*Fajr* Prayer," "First Fast," "Jihana," "Philosophies of Yemeni Shops," "Sa'ada"
Red Cedar: "Sinbad"
Red Weather: "The Deaf-Mutes at the Teashop," "Since You Left al-Hudaydah," "Al-Mukalla" (previously titled "Sestina"), "Hijrah" (previously titled "What Keeps Us")
River Styx: "Malarial," "Requiem for al-Mocha"
The Southern Review: "Can"

Thanks to *Tigertail Annual VII: Three By Three* for publishing the chapbook *Month of Honey, Month of Missiles*, which contains poems in this collection. And to the Anderson Center for Interdisciplinary Studies, Colrain Poetry Conference, Lake Region Arts Council, McKnight Foundation, Mark, Kevin, Kurt, and Shukry, I express my deepest gratitude.

The first *hadith* appearing as epigraph was translated by Ezzeddin Ibrahim and Denys Johnson-Davies. It originally appeared in *An-Nawawi's Forty Hadith* (Salimiah, Kuwait: International Islamic Federation of Student Organizations, 1982). The second *hadith* appearing as an epigraph is adapted from Muhammad Muhsin Khan's translation of *Hadith 671,* Book 59, Volume 5 of *Sahih Al-Bukhari* (Medina, Saudi Arabia: Dar al-Fikr).

FIRST EDITION

Cover Art by Andrew Gifford. *Mosque in Sanaa,* oil on panel, 9" x 10" Andrew Gifford's art may be found online at www.jmlondon.com.
Author Photo by Ama Frederickson.
Book & Cover Design by Christine Holbert.

LIBRARY OF CONGRESS CATALOGING-IN-PUBLICATION DATA

Frederickson, Yahya.
  [Poems. Selections]
  The Gold Shop of Ba-'Ali : poems / by Yahya Frederickson.—First Edition.
    pages cm
  ISBN 978-0-9911465-2-9 (alk. paper)
  I. Title.
  PS3606.R43718A6 2014
  811'.6—dc23
                        2013045681

for Fathia

CONTENTS

I

II

III

IV

كن في الدنيا كأنك غريب أوعابرسبيل

Be in this world as if you are a stranger or a wayfarer.

—*The Prophet Muhammad*

أتاكم أهل اليمن هم أرق أفئدة وألين قلوبا
الإيمان يمان والحكمة يمانية

The people of Yemen have come to you, and they are gentler
and softer-hearted. Belief is Yemeni, and wisdom is Yemeni . . .

—*The Prophet Muhammad*

I

CROSSING

Bab al-Sabah, Old Sana'a

Dry since my arrival, the riverbed this morning
        sparkles with blue water bottles
and plastic bags the hue of coral.

Downstream, Japanese pickups sink into dust
        beneath pyramids of tinder,
each load enough to brown a week of bread.

A flock of fat-tailed sheep lip leafless stems
        while their shepherd hawks hides,
brethren of his own matted coat.

A boy without pants or sandals
        pees into the ravine before wandering
back to the *souq*, where truck horns vie

for position, forward the only direction.
        Likewise I enter, accepting greetings
from a trachea hanging over the brim

of a gutbucket poised on a matron's veiled head.
        Morning of goodness, it nods,
as I stumble over yesterday's hooves strewn about.

Morning of fragrance, it nods, as I smell sheep livers
        cursing from vats of exhausted oil.
To earn a living, all a seller needs is a word

and the throat to wield it. Let mine answer why
        I am in this life so far from my own,
why I enter every day, no desire to buy.

PHILOSOPHIES OF YEMENI SHOPS

Shop of *Sharshaf*s

Whenever she comes to buy, it's night.
I sell by texture without touching.
Floral: a chance meeting in a garden.
Geometric: no room for joking,
an unseen face without lines.
Plain: for the tender daughter
learning to use this tailored dusk.
Enter without fear—I'll never plead,
never steal. This dark Eden is
a covenant too precious to risk.

Shop of Sweets

Stacked cubes of gelatinous red
and green, mounds of orange puffs,
yellow sprinkles, waxy taffy slabs.
Mangled forks, battered tin plates.
The world's rejects collect here:
the scarred, the lonely, the foreign.
Side by side on the narrow bench,
they watch the news on my small TV,
tamp the last forkful into dry crumbles,
sip bitter coffee from chipped cups
long after the sugar has left their mouths.

Butcher Shop

He was a Turk. As rebel cannon
pummeled his outpost, he saw red
lizards skittering from stone windows
and knew it meant an end.
After the wars he stayed, bought a cleaver
and a gutted room. Each day, a fresh
head hung from the hook on his door.
His forearms were known for their whiteness,
but the smell of opened bodies was unmistakably
the same. More accurate than planets,
my grandfather's system has become mine.

Shop of Buta-Gas Canisters

People have been gathering since dawn,
a rare, silent line. Predators and skeletons
together at this drying fuel hole.
Children sprawl in ripped wheelbarrows.
Old women hold their faces in the shade.
The man who sears beans in the restaurant
will wheel away six. Mark your place
in the queue with a spent canister.
As we pitch fresh steel from the truck,
hear the taut *ping*, the sour chill
of butane ready to drink spark.

SINBAD

I have wasted the morning dreaming
about eyes not in need of mascara,
about the wind that films my table
with the peaks of eroding mountains.

I must leave my apartment for a while,
get some air, perhaps in a distant market,
somewhere I won't have to haggle. On the curb,
I stir the air with a finger, the signal

for Ring Road. Buses bluster past,
their drivers gesturing to me *enough*.
The bodies stuffed against the windshields
tell me they are not lying.

Finally a bus halts its rattling,
letting me climb, crouch, and squat
adjacent the door, behind the driver,
where every face can't search mine for answers.

I do not care to be read today.
Along Ring, shops splay open their doors,
revealing booty: mutton on hooks,
shelves of jarred honey, carpets from Turkey.

The seat beside me will stay empty
until the last unlucky boob has no option
but sit beside me and be ignored.
And here he comes now, a ragged old man

dragging sacks of potatoes and onions
into my poisonous garden.
From the corner of my eye, I can see
he's gazing at me like a rustic.

He'll ask me my name and my country,
my age, marital status, and salary,
no question off-limits. He'll ask
for my address, and days later

he'll be banging my door for a visa
as if I were a kind ambassador,
as if I could pull any string
in this loopy world. He adjusts his onions,

which have shifted against my ankle,
and turns to me. His mouth opens,
but what comes is a voice I remember
from old films: in gruff Brooklynese

he says sorry to bother me. And he plunges
the blue anchor of his hand into mine.
Soon I am the one who is asking for his saga
of leaving young and returning old.

I ask and ask for more, until at his alley,
he bids the bus stop, and it does. Hoisting his sacks,
he croaks *g'bye*, the kind you turn to watch
drift away, the kind used to lasting a lifetime.

HERBS

Bab al-Sho'ub, Old Sana'a

On a stone doorstep she sells little bundles of herbs from her family's garden. She wears the intricate-print *sitara* of the women who live in this ancient capital as if it were a remote village. Though a row of herb-women sit on this market street, I know her from the others, for her eyes are a mountain village at night, a pack of wild dogs growling in the periphery. As I near, she is always the first to look away. What does it mean to look away, to look at all, or not look? I ask her the prices of her herbs. When I first saw her, I asked her the name of each herb, straining to listen amid the market racket, the muffle of her veil, and the smell of smoke from Safia, the old widow upstairs, who set onto the embers of her hookah a soggy ball of tobacco, the smoldering tang descending, tendrilling around us. Every Thursday afternoon, the herb-woman's husband stands at my door with a bundle of *qat* and a thermos of incense-water. We spend hours chatting in Arabic about money, food, and politics until our private shadows loom larger than the shadows of buildings, until the night is perfumed with names: *baqdoonis . . . na'na' . . . rayhan*—names formed for me by his wife's mouth beneath cloth.

6

RESTAURANT OF THE VIETNAMESE HALF-CASTES

Agriculture Street, Sana'a

Coming before noon ensures shrimp, coconut milk, pineapple tang, rice more Asian than Arabian. As my plate arrives at my sidewalk card table, so does Ali, who asks if he may join me. *Of course*, I lie. He has learned to cower. Working for the American company was good, he says, until an accident short-circuited half of his face. I know that half intimately: it's the half that sees into me, that will soon discover I am useless to him, that I cannot turn the lead of his life into gold.

After the meal, as we sip sweet tea, Hamoud bangs a chair down at our table. In English tempered by movies and rap, he's cursing his father's homeland, its soldiers who don't like what might be hiding behind his car windows' purple tint. The next time they stop him, they'll throw him in jail, so he's scraping it off with a razor blade. But when a flock of *Vietnami* Girl Guides passes by, he exaggerates them a salute. One of the girls smiles back, her satchel clutched against her chest like a shield.

The restaurant fills with men from the Ministry of Agriculture across the street. They wear Western suits, leave food on their plates, and argue loudly for the bill. Abdu counts their cash at the counter inscrutably. After they leave, he dumps their scraps together into a bag for the little beggar girl waiting on the step, who grasps the handles in her gray-green hands and strains away, the scraps marbling inside the plastic.

7

CAN

Can a can can a can? the students of linguistics quiz me, giggling as if they've heard the most delicious gossip. They are students of Dr. D. Thakur, or D.T., the Indian professor who has been teaching here since the university was built. With his thick glasses, Brylcreemed silver hair, and calm demeanor, he's as guru as can be in a country of Muslims. Surrounded by his disciples in the inner sanctum of his flat, he claps his hands and says, *Madame, sweets.* His wife parts the curtain, setting before them a tray of petit-fours and tamarind juice.

Can a can can a can? they bubble while I scowl. Late for my own lecture, I'm walking past the Faculty of Science, where the skeleton of a whale or huge fish, probably from the Red Sea, is displayed. It must be similar to whatever swallowed Yunus, the claustrophobic story familiar to all People of the Book. Behind me, the hedges of red geraniums are in bloom. Oh, to be the lucky gardener of the university grounds, day in and day out slaking the thirst of things that bloom and bear fruit! No wonder young women sit on the benches nearby, drawing Seven-Up from cool green bottles, through bright plastic straws, to their lips.

Can a can can a can? the jerks keep asking, and I'm guessing that it is a grammatical miracle, a secret code they expect me to know. What I know for sure is that it is the stupidest question I've ever heard. Over their silly grins, I notice male students at the main gate surrendering their daggers to the soldier. They'll get the daggers back after class. Last year during final exams, the soldier's pet buzzard, loose from its tether, hopped into my classroom. My students slapped its beak with their test papers until it squawked and, like I do when confounded by a puzzle, flustered away.

QAHWA AL-BAIDHANI

In al-Baidha, the fields enter the elixir, grain
added to blond and dark brown beans. I'm invited
to a wedding there next week. The young groom
has returned from America for marriage. I'm sitting
next to him now in a friend's *diwan*, our elbows
sharing a red velvet pillow. He shows me a small album
of photos from America. In every shot, he straddles
the polished curves of sports cars. He found a place to love
the sun and all of its maidens. Next Thursday evening,
he will marry a child who has never left al-Baidha.
His American babe clicked frame after frame as if
the more she clicked, the more he would stay.
But the choice isn't all his. Decisions have already been made
by two families, by a place where coffee tastes soft and light
in the mouth of the young bride, who sips one last
cup before her village collapses in the wheat.

DUQQ

I believe only the desert can know the aridity
of cardamom, coffee, and ginger. In his small *diwan*,
Firas and I sip *duqq* with his distant relatives,
who have come from their village for medicine,
work, or maybe an official stamp. I don't pry.
The poster above my head shows Saddam Hussein
atop a white stallion, greeting a clapping throng.
A cousin asks about America's motives as if
I am my country and he is his. My Arabic,
tinder-dry, heats the room. But beyond the door,
Firas's mother is listening. She hears me ask
about the drink she prepared. I sip until the faces
of relatives eclipse and it is time to excuse myself.
At the door, Firas places an aromatic sack
into my hand, recites the instructions his mother
gave him to give me for steeping the night.

THE LAST TIME

The last time I hung out with Ahmad was after we'd been at a teashop, talking about music over milky tea. I'm feeling sleepy, but Ahmad says, *The night is still early. I've got a couple of guitars at home, and my wife and children are out of town.* I cave, so we walk to his flat. At the gate, a car is parked. *Oh no,* he mutters. *Salih.*

Inside, we're met by Ahmad's older cousin Salih, an officer in the military. Another cousin, I forget his name, is there too, sitting in the corner of the *diwan*, his cheek bulging with *qat*, his hand busy with a cigarette. And at the other end of the room, a woman sits on the floor. She is poised like an empress, her straight back, her confident smile. She is dressed in a gown of turquoise satin, and her hair is wrapped in a scarf of sparkling gold. All of us sit before her in silent adoration.

Salih leaves the room. When he returns, he is no longer wearing his olive uniform but a white terrycloth bathrobe, his belly protruding over the cinched belt. Our presence will not alter his objective. I cringe to picture it. Our queen looks too fresh to be a prostitute, too comfortable to be a victim. For her delights, how much will he pay?

Salih glares at us; we've wasted too much of his time. The thinner cousin is staying put in his corner, maybe to watch, maybe to wait his own sloppy turn. Ahmad leads me out of the *diwan* and down the hall, to a small room whose shelves are stacked high with American CDs, whose cushions cradle two guitars. I start a slow blues shuffle while Ahmad thumb-strums something sad and Spanish. Our songs don't merge. We try a Bob Dylan tune that both of us know, but even that is hopeless: inside the room closed tight as a small fist, our discordant notes crumble onto the floor. We can't even keep time anymore.

ALL-NIGHT TEASHOP

Having tallied the day's cracks,
Majnoon sleeps on the sidewalk
with his soiled blanket and tin can.

A *qat* chewer spits his desires into the street.
He orders a glass of milk tea,
strokes the softness of his own soft cheek.

Inside, behind a squad of blenders,
the sandwich boy furrows out
the soft guts of a bun.

Under the lone fluorescent bulb,
an army transport rattles to a halt,
emptying its cargo of young soldiers.

Their carbines sleep across their laps
as they devour sandwiches of jam
and cheese, glasses of mango juice.

And what am I? Not a tourist,
not a spy, not an oil man looking to hire.
I offer no opportunities,

nothing, except maybe
the forgiveness I see, no greater wish
in the world than tea.

THE DEAF-MUTES AT THE TEASHOP

The waiter no longer puzzles over orders made
with hands and empty glasses.

When two hands tell a joke,
laughter billows from their palms.

When they talk politics,
their knuckles become subversive.

In the street, children collect a pile
of wastepaper, search for a

discarded lighter to float ash
and a ribbon of smoke into the night.

Finishing their second orbit of tea,
my stars arc between the tight circles

of smoke and children, between
the constellations of chairs

from which other men loudly curse.
Everyone hears.

II

JIHANA

The grenade the tribe lobbed into
your compound was not for you
but your landlord.

When glass rained in, no one was home
but his wife, who spent the rest of the night
shuddering on the kitchen floor.

Remember the nurse who converted,
married a local man whose pistol
prayed harder than he. She

looked for faith, but found
his outlaw town. Nevertheless,
she embraced, and stayed.

Besides grapes and guns,
the *souq* sells whatever trucks
smuggle across the border.

Learn how to haggle,
how to hide in a private chamber
what is precious.

Tonight in Jihana,
under lights garlanded between houses,
a family works a man

into its life like a dance with knives,
while cousins fire their rifles
at the sky.

SA'ADA

I come with foreign language, no jobs,
a curiosity long useless, which carries me through
the big door, the *souq* of Jews,
who trust me more than neighbors.
A face like mine airlifted their relatives
to Jerusalem, while the elderly stayed behind,
soldering hinges on ornate boxes,
hanging baubles from chain mail.
Ask why. Will they crimp words together,
Hebrew and Arabic, to explain?

I'd heard about the checkpoints, the searches.
When the soldier boarding the bus looked at me,
he saw *kaafir*, smuggler, spy.
He confiscated my stamped passport
to show his captain before grunting it back.
The dust devils spinning in the distance
were tribal artillery, not *jinn*.
The rest of the passengers kept defoliating *qat*,
smoking Kamarans, every window shut tight.
Any draft would mar the tender longing
they lose themselves in while riding
over brown lunar crags.

Pink and aqua plastic bags snap open and soar
around me as I walk back millennia
on the Old City wall. Suddenly, it crumbles,
the thick-walled houses part, and I'm standing
in the dusty surf of a sea of garbage.
A shirtless man digs out of the waves.
What is it you want from coral? he asks.
A tribal dream? To be desired by dark eyes?

In the waiting room of al-Salaam Hospital,
a veiled mother nurses her baby.
After his shift, the Sudanese chief surgeon
will go to the rec room. Taking a chipped cue,
he'll sink every ball on the table.
Where have my choices brought me?
At the next checkpoint, what will I surrender?
No photocopied documents, no *bakhsheesh*,
no reason to be here. I've learned the futility
of proof, a commodity no one hoards.

ON SABIR MOUNTAIN

After tea, Mr. Mohandas asks if I would like to ascend. He must check the progress of the development project today. I follow him downstairs, where the servant who brought us tea is now the chauffeur poised at the wheel of the company Land Rover. We drive up, past the house of the man rich enough to demand the city's asphalt streets meet him at his gate, then up the dusty switchbacks until Ta'izz shrinks into the valley. On the slope a group of stonecutters ties a block on a man's back so he can walk it down. They offer us tea from the one small glass they share, but we decline. Up, up, we cut through terraced fields. The women of this mountain are storied. Proud as queens, they depend on no man to provide. In marriage, they command the highest dowries in the land, their lips grinning around teeth of gold! The Land Rover turns into the construction site, splitting the crowd that has already gathered. By the way the hand of Mr. Mohandas is shaken and kissed, I can tell the visit will take time. In the valley far below, the city has all but submerged. The only sounds are a water pump's chugging diesel, and laughter—for a cluster of young girls has spotted me. Already they know how little I comprehend. Village-bright, their dresses billow in the wind, so I ask *mumkin surah?*, maybe a photograph? But they shrink away, hiding their mouths with the ends of their scarves, as their mothers would do. In a few years, suitors will ruin themselves for their small hands. Uphill, Mr. Mohandas motions me to return. The inspection is complete. During our long idle down, everything is as silent as time. Occasionally, I see an iridescent lizard warming itself on a stone. Down, down, into the city's loftiest precinct, where children frolic in the streets, swishing their shirts and shawls through the air. It is not a greeting for us, but for the diaphanous insects that they are catching in the folds. To my surprise, they bite with glee into each abdomen, which, like this day, must be swollen with indescribable nectar.

REQUIEM FOR AL-MOCHA

for Jenny

Long gone the coffee, the storehouses
reeking of cinnamon, saffron, incense.
We walk the barren coast as clouds
crash and try to rain salt. They can't.

For 300 years, brick has been sinking,
rows of black stones askew in grit,
houses of dead merchants reduced
to rafters gray goats clitter across.

Minaret or lighthouse, rubble is rubble,
the barber reasons, swigging smuggled whiskey
in his shop's solitary chair. Ships
bring him more bottles than heads.

Every night, the landlady sleepwalks
up the stairs, stands in your doorway,
stares out from beneath the yellow bulb.
Her family escaped, but she's afraid to hate.

Even babies born dry and hard as dolls
fight for this life. Perhaps the placentas
mothers bury in sand do bring luck.
Luck of your hands, of any history at all.

CATTLE FROM ETHIOPIA

Relentless as minutes,
the sea stampedes the brim
of a rickety Djibouti ship.
In the night's warm waves,
cows know only east, and swim.
Today they rest like uprooted palms.

Stare into an open bovine eye
as crabs tunnel through flesh, orifice
to orifice, clicking diligent mandible
against mandible, crabs exiting
in panicked battalions, poking
eyestalks from sloping foam.

How many teeth to make a necklace?
What could be done with horn,
should it twist loose?
In a homeland not far,
people roll onto shore
with gaping holes.

A soldier offers
mango juice, sandwich cookies,
cigarettes. He's returning
to his village of thatch and fish
where children, in hot sand,
bury everything they hear.

MALARIAL

A boy sits beside me, watching the ebb
and flow of my face. Arabic words bob
along the surface, an alien accent:
'ammi   'atoora   al-Hudaydah
as cheap amber perfume moistens my wrist.

Minutes ago, days ago, the sea silenced
a scream. A baked salt plain cracked
beneath my feet as I followed fishermen
walking somewhere home,
stalked a small mosque onto the horizon.

A man plods toward me, his hard toes
separating, sinking like a turtle's into dunes.
He brings water from palm groves, warm juice.
Reminiscent of peach and pine, mango
is my own pungent past.

On the beach, an old man hacks melons open,
sings wedding songs. Look: sunset, fishermen
walking back on water, carrying streamers
of dangling fish. They've come to devour
sweet red flesh.

No reason to remember names, places.
Only the nectarous juice running down
the brown cords of their arms, the fever
their foreheads press into damp sand
for the God who brought them back.

SINCE YOU LEFT AL-HUDAYDAH

for Wayne

Tea at the Borg Terrace still comes slow as sleep,
briny, in china from a defunct inn. I can still sit for hours
watching couples stroll below, in People's Garden,
shifting like chess pieces over the lawn
in their long white and black gowns.

I spent the morning searching
for the coldest mango juice in town, an excuse
to languish in rooms with frantic ceiling fans.
Where I finally found it, the proprietor's left eye
bulged red. I wonder if you'd searched too,
found both eye and juice.

In the market, I tried to shoot
the tiers of displayed fruits, the most
colors I've seen that weren't Somali clothes.
But from the middle stall a broken voice said no,
no photos.

A woman you knew claimed a bright green line
lingers on the horizon after sunset
as if the sea would allow the submerged orb
one final bleary glow. On relentlessly hot nights,
she entered the rooms of sleeping men,
and explained. On those nights, you dreamed
of blue foxes eating their young.

I remember your daily trips to the post office,
the wilted envelopes from home. After reading them,
you floated whatever they held in the tepid waves
until shadows grew bold beneath your feet.
How far away love remains.

THE BUS TO ADEN

stops in a village whose name
no one knows. Time for lunch.
In the seats in front of me,
passengers stir from their naps,
from their dreams of what traveling brings,
and stagger down the bus steps
then up the cement steps
into the open-front restaurant,

which fills instantly. The family
of waiters echoes our orders back
to the kitchen: trays of flaky bread,
tin plates of rice, sheep heads
yellowing in broth. After the meal,
our throats blossom with sweet red tea.
Though I try to consume quickly,

I am the last back on board, where
passengers have begun swapping
shopping stories, crinkling baby clothes
encased in cellophane, smoothing the bolts
of cloth bought for aunts. I can tell
our driver is from Aden, for his free hand
speaks with an excitement only subversives have.
Something must always be brought home.

KRATER

When they dynamited the ancient bridge,
Shamsan bone rained. Ever since,
the hole opens more. Buildings born
in a year spend dozens dying. Neither mosque,
colonial cross, nor Hindu shrine will wail.

Evening in Seera, a hi-fi speaker
throbs Euro disco over the stagnant bay.
From a transistor at the Sinalco stand,
tinny Egyptian. The sullen cashier
can change metal to paper to shell.

What we have to lose are gutted
blue Hungarian buses, doctored concrete.
The next conqueror Allah will allow.
Look at yourself, sweating on the pocked asphalt.
To scour your life, it'll take lava.

BALHAF

On the beach before the sultan's ruins
lies the skeleton of a *dhow*
picked clean of aromatic gum.
Delicate white crabs gesticulate the shore
into peaks and fine-grained pores.

Fishermen spread ripped nets with their toes,
and mend. No need to teach the young the work,
no need for words, for ears
near the bludgeoning ocean.

Flamingoes stampede into heat
as a pickup loaded down with dry sharks
rounds the volcanic hill.
A broken Marxist curses his outboard.

A look into the veiled world of shells reveals
scallop, spiral, mantle—forms
shifting in the mind, emerging,
a face whose love isn't returned, lip
on lip, lip on teeth.

The red skate gliding through the shallows
I'll tail to the breakers
until the smooth moon glistens everything briny,
hideous, everything skin.

AL-MUKALLA

In the packed pariah taxi from Aden,
        I traveled with nothing but gold
wind blowing in my face for half a day.
        Neither a cool palm
nor the shadow of one crooned.
        Speed kept in check the prodding flies,
but nothing reins in the humps
        of hungry, galloping sand
rolling over the sole road.
        We played leapfrog with sharks
nose-down in a pickup box
        until we heard the chugging generators

of al-Mukalla. Only a few hours of power per day,
        so every home generates
its own: the youngest son is sent upstairs with benzene,
        and the rooms return gold,
a flood of soft light in which women unveil,
        relax, away from the sharks
of the outer world who think themselves sun gods.
        Henna-ed palms
release fists of flowers. Long, oiled hair
        has once again escaped airborne sand.
All the day's *jinn* blur, and pictureless walls
        allow angels to freely fly.

Can't help but be blessed. And when the rooms
        are reentered by flies,
you know another warm morning has come.
        No need for generators
until the sun has wilted the day's hope
        of weightlessness and laughter, the sandy
throats of fishermen as they slice
        through salt backbones. Roe, golden,
is saved for those in need of delicacies

slightly grotesque: the tall palms'
orgies of sticky dates from an inland valley,
the hammerhead shark's

dorsal fin. Too much trust in folk aphrodisiacs.
Though not yet old, I rarely shark
through anything anymore. No desire for
uncommitted love, for drugs inducing flight,
floating me hysterical over my own bones.
Some say the ropy lines of my palm
unravel too soon; friends Honduran as well as Adeni
have sworn that generations
springing from our loins will verify the truth of astrology.
But people since Golden
Age Greece have sworn the same, and all that remain
are shadows. I believe sand

to be more accurate. See how it covers the Empty
Quarter so perfectly, identical sand
mounds all the way to the Emirates. Bedouins know.
In Land Cruisers they're the sharks
smuggling goods across unpatrolled borders.
A serious old smith makes their gold
mooria's bare round beads, and the big,
dangly crescent earrings that city women fly
past on their way to the latest Gulf styles.
Fondling the smooth globes generates
hazy pictures of India, Aden, Ethiopia—
places like sable fingers on the palm

of the Indian Ocean. Influence is so difficult
to understand. The oppressive palm
of an ancient tyrant we accept so effortlessly.
Today, lines drawn in the sand
are crossed by foreign missiles. Satellite dishes
on the roofs of mud homes. Generators
ensure them of satellite TV, blue French movies.

In my dreams, a technological shark
swallows every wire, every chip, then disappears
   like Socotran soldiers flying
to their island home with the help of *jinn*.
   Other than this apocalypse, hope remains gold:

hopes of snaking sewage through a verdant palm maze,
   of leading white sharks
into a shallow bay of sand. All that is left to know
   are the motives of flies
filling our eyes, and how a generator's drone
   convinces dry lips to know gold.

III

REVOLUTION DAY

On the roof of *Bayt* Abu-Talib, I'm eating grapes
and reading the explosions over Tahrir Square.
Liars, they proclaim *this is yours*. But there's something
about their sounds, so distant, so muffled.

A few floors below, my friends light a candle
in the blackout, whisper the latest gossip
into the lapping light. And in the cobbled street,
a kid with a giddy coat hanger is chasing

a pack of dogs past the shop where I buy food.
Now its blue metal doors are padlocked,
but mornings an old woman works there, the only

merchant I truly trust. Can't count. Can't read.
I'm not sure what I believe. The last
turgid grape spurts between my teeth.

POETRY LESSON

What I learned about poetry in Yemen,
        I learned at a sidewalk café off of Zubairi Street,
one of the main streets in Sana'a
        named after the poet who fomented revolution with rhyme,

where I'm finishing off a plate of butterflied chicken,
        the aroma of garlic and lemon marinade mixing
with the smoke fanned by a piece of cardboard box,
        the grill right there on the sidewalk,

when a ragged old man tramps by looking like a *bedouin*,
        a holy man in hard plastic shoes,
banging his walking staff on the pavement and reciting poetry,
        which, even though I can't

understand, I know is poetry. Maybe the smell
        of the grilled food caught his attention,
but he doesn't stop singing his poetry as loud
        as his lungs will allow to the waiters, cooks,

and whoever else is listening, which I am
        as I'm standing there paying my bill, and now
he's dancing—banging his staff in rhythm,
        stamping a couple steps forward, couple steps back,

BANG!—I've got to admit that I am feeling it too,
        so I put my arms up in the air like his,
he grasps my wrist, and suddenly we're dancing together,
        the waiters smiling

and clapping as we go back and forth, *BANG!*
        in front of the restaurant,
until the end nears, the big finish,
        everyone is standing and cheering, I've got to

buy him lunch, I mean I've just got to, because
        when was the last time I tasted
poetry like that, not just a cool mint swirl in the brain,
        but a wash of chile in the marrow?

So I slam some *rials* down on the counter
        for another platter of chicken and rice,
but he's got no time to sit and eat,
        so the waiters bag it up for him, and off he goes

toward the city center, his bag of food
        swinging from one hand, his staff in the other,
his hard shoes clopping away, my day
        swinging from his neck like a medallion.

EMBRACE

Beyond my wooden shutters,
the world hums and buzzes.

The tall houses nearby
spill their secrets: a toddler

howling through bars
after a mother's cuff,

an aluminum lid
clanging onto its kettle,

an old man and an old woman
quarreling without teeth,

a girl on the roof scowling
laundry onto a clothesline.

I walk through the Old City
and the New, to the university,

where my student Marwan
tells me his dream.

I saw you, my teacher,
and you were Muslim,

he says, handing me a pamphlet
rife with misspellings.

Last night, who worried more
about my eternity than he?

Like this, I fall in love
with every pure

but imperfect intention:
every stone staircase

with uneven steps,
every mud wall built

to lead me away,
every peel and pit

strewn in the fruit *souq*
because the buyer couldn't wait,

every bent key
to open a gate.

FIRST FAST

Three hundred *muezzin*s are born,
pulse, and fade. That, the pattern
worked into the bones of those
living between stone floors, bones
that navigate every blind corner,
every catacomb. Today is the seventh
of my first Ramadan, the seventh day

I have ever fasted. I am sitting
in my barren, ancient kitchen
near Bab al-Sho'ub, gulping water,
guessing the right time to end.
I've lived in Old Sana'a long enough
to decipher its alleys, gates, markets,
and the Great Mosque's long

windowless walls, its beggars sagging
around the big door, the order of red rugs
and white pillars deep within.
I've seen how quickly breeze
becomes storm, how quickly children
sense something in a foreigner's eyes
that makes each small hand clutch stone.

I want to weave branches
into a wooden ceiling strong enough
to support another floor, another dream,
to know why, between howling night
and honking daylight, there's a hush
that makes the world weak.
I fear what I might mean.

FAJR PRAYER

From half-sleep, hear the spinning,
the whirlwind consuming the city,
gathering momentum from each *muezzin*,
turning night into roosters and twilight.

Cold water breaks the hard corners
of eyes, rinses the pouches of ancient mouths,
the cracked soles intimate with mountains.

The sun will rise again between Satan's horns,
the Sudanese remembers, unlocking his shop
to more exhaust and grease.

No matter how dismal, never curse dawn:
no way of knowing what will open
when the world blossoms purple
and the worn streets rise and testify.

LETTER

Consider the foreigners who came before us, the Slav who doctored the final imam deep within the city's walls. The sun rose and fell without shadows. Today, decades later, Sana'a explodes, clouds of white taxi vans waiting for seconds to tick away in the traffic soldier's gun, for lights to flinch before surrendering green. On the corner of Zubairi and Ring, beggars without legs scuff from car to car. A battered wheelbarrow bears a hag small and fragile enough to be a newborn, swathed in rags and wool batting. I miss watching the hawks from my top-floor flat spiral down through the lavender sunset to roost in spires of eucalyptus and pine. Are you making good use of the moon? Mine still eclipses daily. But I've learned to leave celestial bodies to God. And I've discovered I can sleep anywhere: on a sand dune beside the Red Sea, in the quiet corner of a mosque in Tunisia, on a metal airport bench at LAX. Perhaps what I'm trying to say is goodbye. And don't worry. Even a coyote knows it won't be alone forever.

JINN

1

In mid-sentence, my friend's jaws
rip open, from teeth to trachea,
the cords of his neck locked in a vise.
Slithering out of the eclipse,
English, a tongue he never learned.
A voice gurgles from beneath asphalt:
What has drowned in your heart?

2

Leave your house at midnight.
Besides cold soldiers slouching
in open-backed transports, the only
other life burns within the dogs
whimpering and prancing
through the empty market,
where blue metal doors suffocate
the rant of Hindi gold.

3

Wasef leads me through doors
and curtains, to an inner chamber.
My father has got a patient, he says,
and disappears. In a distant room,
I hear Sheikh 'Uthman shouting
the Qur'an at something. I hear
a neck growling back at a cane.
Wasef brings me biscuits and milk tea,
sits practicing his English with me
until his father bids him bring water.
When he returns, he is grinning.
The jinni likes me. And he asked me,
"Wasef, who is that sitting with you,
who is that stranger with the honey-green eyes?"

THE STONE POLISHER

Indian healers, I hear,
hoard the deepest, reddest *'aqeeq*.
Rub one into a wound,
and it'll halt blood.

But he hasn't time for such hearsay.
Unfolding a paper envelope,
he spills its droplets onto the counter.
Anything is possible, if Allah wills,

he says, and returns to his pillow
in the corner of the *samsara*,
his low workbench, his jeweler's glass,
and the stone on which
he is engraving Allah's name.

IV

RITE

From the grand *diwan* of al-Ahmar
where women beat tambourines
and ululate with mouths I'll never see,

you float down the dark stairs,
filling the corridor with layer
upon layer of veil, an apparition

moving toward me without word
or touch. Sheikh Abdullah's Land Cruiser
will whisk us along the belt

of streetlights around this city,
in whose heart I pulse, in whose mouth
my tongue has learned a new language.

Our convoy of cars honks
with the promise of migrating swans.
In the seats behind us, the shadows

of your best friends and their daughters
hold whispered conversations.
Tonight, I know you less than ever.

But in the crevice between us, our hands
have found one another. We will learn
that love means what we have begun.

THE DAY AFTER

Dar al-Hamd Hotel, Sana'a

The day after he missed my wedding, my American father still lies flat on his back in bed. Perhaps the change of altitude was the culprit, perhaps his first in-country meal, a tepid five-star buffet. I turn the television on for him, forgetting that the sole channel doesn't air until mid-afternoon. Even then, the anchorman's voice will be muted.

Through the open window, we can hear the old goatherd below in the garden of the last imam, scuttling his charges out of the lettuce, scuttling preschoolers out of the peach trees. I watch a pickup stop at the kitchen's service door. If my father saw the driver's fingers gripping the delivered loaves, he would sicken again.

Yesterday at the groom's luncheon, while my guests feasted on *tabbouleh* and roasted goat, I greeted them, passing from the room of the powerful, to the room of the common, to the room of the unknown. That is where I sat down, surrounded by their silent, tired lives. I cleaned every morsel from my plate, then joined them in staring at the floor.

Now, the sun, reaching its zenith, dismisses school. Girls uniformed in slate coats and white scarves step single-file down the garden path. The fields flanking them seem to change daily: yesterday onion, today lettuce, tomorrow carrot. My father sits up to spoon a bowl of broth.

Into tomorrow's bowl, he'll float a torn loaf. And the day after, he'll step slowly up the irregular stone stairs to the top floor, where I'll creak open the door of the imam's private *diwan*. Pulling back a curtain, he'll gaze upon this ancient land. I'll wonder what my father is thinking.

AL-KHUZAIMAH CEMETERY

I follow my wife into the vast, dusty grid.
We are newlyweds walking to the grave
of her father, whom I never met
but doubt would've approved our union.

He was a bricklayer until an allergy
to cement sent him home. His two daughters
began working in offices, buying for him
what comforts remained: sweets, cigarettes,

a television, big and Japanese.
He read news magazines and kept alive
a sad, abnormally large dog that ambled back
every night for scraps and slept at his door.

Locating his concrete slab, my wife prays
for mercy. Her eyes well up, the same tears
she'll hide from me in the coming years
remembering how far we are from this field of hearts.

SECESSION

I

As anti-aircraft guns begin their nightly ripping of zinc,
we gather the judge's paralyzed wife in a blanket, lug her
downstairs into the windowless stone hallway. Clutching
the corner over her shoulder, I slip into her eye, which has
surrendered to the unearthly gravity and indirect light in
which she exists. What fear hasn't she already known? Her
husband's government fell hard. Her husband, in his seventies,
took a second wife. Soon the flood started moving up her
body, bathing more and more of her in a motionless blue
not unlike the sky over their ancestral village. After sunset,
we hunker down around her. *Minda . . . Minda . . . Minda . . .*
she burbles for her Filipina nurse. Her mouth can no longer
pronounce the name of her daughter, the one whispering
to her now through worried fingers. She can't erase her
husband's eyes, their fierce blue rings around brown, though
she submerged them years ago in her memory's cistern.

2

Heat lightning to the south could easily be artillery, the same flashing pulse miming mortars fired skyward. The news anchorman talks of traitors. The dead are never shown. Rumor has it the meat lockers in Ta'izz are full of frozen soldiers the government doesn't want to cart home. In Thamar, separatist forces leveled the electric plant before being leveled in turn. We've reached a point of not knowing, somewhere between our house and our neighbor's stone hall where we wait under blankets for dawn, recite the shortest Qur'anic *surahs*, and trust little else. Perhaps the driveway's unraked piles of crushed stone resemble the hills of Hadramaut, the volcanic rock and white dunes enemies know like the backs of unburnt hands; 30,000, maybe 80,000 hands. The lightning animates the trees in Zihra's orchard. We have never met him, nor seen what kind of fruit the lush leaves conceal, but I am certain it's sweeter than anything flesh could know.

3

Another night snubs another day. Sunset prayer says *peace*, covering a blanket of hand-woven hair over the evening's whispers. I'm walking home beside the sewage trickling down the middle of a mud alley. Moons of stained glass blush from top-floor rooms, where witnesses listen to the news guaranteeing the government forces Heaven. They and their families will drink from its flooding rivers. Meanwhile, our driveway slopes away like an arched back. A boy stood there yesterday, pointing his pellet gun at the sky. A tiny ball of down perching on the TV aerial sensed the rushing metal. Children know much about war. Doubtless, death will be promised to many little boys when birds turn a deep enduring blue, the color of cobalt towers, of the stars flickering above hollow bones. The neighbor's children have fallen asleep, but their dreams crash like cymbals.

4

One of these days a rain of rockets will unsnap the minds
of street dogs. Many believers will turn palms down, revert
to scripted shells, black yarn tied around ankles. I'm not
afraid of what Allah wills. I try to stop boys from pegging
rocks at the dogs, their minor moment of power over
fangs. I'm relieved when the pack struggles out through
our metal gate and flees into the street. They'll be back at
night to own the boys. I've shaved my head. The reason, I
say, is the heat. In the south, heads like mine are burning
the arsenal al-'Anad, ripping up carpet from the luxury
hotel lobby, taking what can be gripped. At home, I'm
a soldier who can't satisfy his wife. Twice, I've cried like
fire. Things distant ring a beauty not unlike missiles: fists
buried in feather pillows, water tanks bulging near the
border moments before mortars. In a distant precinct,
an imam speeds up sunset. I have learned it's possible to
distrust and live, to feel absolutely nothing around me.

5

At 9:00, the same hour-long news. Continuous official rhetoric, no sound bytes, no war footage. No analysis of strategy, trajectory, soaring prices. No sign of killing. The president sits at a long table, mouthing directives to military advisors. Each segment ends with a lit Italian chandelier, the sign that the world has never had faith in anything but firelight. My sister-in-law has discovered a cockroach striding along the living room pillows. She runs to the kitchen, comes back pulling a thick black rubber glove onto her right hand like a surgeon. Catching it between thumb and forefinger, she walks briskly to the door, throws the whirling-antennae pinch into the silent twilight. Across the courtyard, we can see the big black Xs our neighbor has taped over her windows to prevent them from shattering. I scoffed at her feeble attempt to save until our windows flew inside.

6

People are piling pillows, mattresses, children into pickups.
They'll drive to waterless villages, set kids in concrete
rooms of second cousins twice removed, and wait. No
one anywhere will be relieved. Pressure from the blasts has
rained plaster and colored glass onto floors. Blue waterfalls
of window glass surge into the street. The judge estimates
his age at 83, based on a time line of dead relatives and tribal
feuds. He knew this neighborhood before the Revolution,
when Jews lived in the sunken houses. I ride with the judge
and his grandson to the explosion site. The soldier at
the roadblock kisses the judge's hand, lets only him pass
through the rubble. Fifteen minutes later, he returns, drops
into my hand a mangled metal clot. It is strong, light, a
piece of the missile housing. The night it fell, dozens of
dogs rumbled in the empty lot opposite the presidential
palace. They bayed in a way I'd never heard before, a way
that made women lock their children indoors, slip buckets
outside to catch the impending storm.

7

Missiles in the Eid of Sacrifice. Few risk praying sunset prayer at mosques near the Republican Palace. However, on Hadda Street the ice cream shop is full of customers. Crowding over the cold cases, veiled girls wait boldly for Syrian pistachio. Young kids shout for brown paper pouches of potato chips, shakers of salt and cayenne. From the rolled-down windows of Land Cruisers, sons of the rich blare Michael Jackson, hope their friends see them smooth as new bullets, bold in the face of missiles. They'll roar down the emptied streets, blurring the blue doors to perfection. All their favorite shops remain open till curfew: music, burgers, videos, mango juice. In the market, what I want is out of stock. No relief from the monotony I've discovered in my mortal home. In a small mosque, old men read *Surat Yaseen* in unison for those whose homes Monday's Scud exploded over them, whose belongings were snatched out of the piles of glass, broken bricks, and bodies, by looters.

54

8

Month of honey, month of missiles. On the way to the neighbor's hallway, I stoop and swim in the clean, purple sky. The Big Dipper has been upturned for months, no sign of dissipation. On Channel One, a man pried from the wreckage praises Allah from a bed in al-Salaam Hospital. Under one mud building, twenty-five bludgeoned. The whitecaps of your nightgown roll toward the warm beach of night. I make plans by praying. Plans with you and falling water, flattened trees, the earth of a different brown country. Whatever manner of flesh will rekindle our blackened bones, Allah can raise it above the pounding, cover it with the coolest mist.

QISHR

On Fridays in Old Sana'a, little boys are dressed
in vests made from sacks of coffee hulls,
the coarse black and white yarns artfully frayed.
Fatima our neighbor has one son and three daughters.
She has been married twice, divorced twice.
The daughters sit on the floor around their mother,
studying the day's lessons. My wife has been with them
since sunset. I've come to escort her home.
My knock on the heavy wooden door is answered
by the release of the latch from within.
I pass through a diaphanous curtain.
No one greets me, but from an inner chamber
I hear female voices. Fatima's voice offers me *qishr*
from a thermos. Take a small cup from the table near the door,
it instructs, before returning to its task. I sip the liquid twilight,
remembering my wedding, the advice my wife
surely received, Fatima's voice explaining the world
from deep within the fortress of her home.

THE GOLD SHOP OF BA-'ALI

al-Mukalla

They step up to the display case, an old father,
his wife, and a daughter newly engaged.
They have come from a hot village.
The father removes an old kerchief from his pocket,
unwraps baubles to trade as they shop

for their daughter's bridal gold. In *Souq al-Nisa'*,
serious buyers come here first. *We've been here
too long to need a sign*, whispers a son of Ba-'Ali.
From the back room the saline odor
of a small, desiccated shark floats forward.

Perhaps tomorrow, after soaking overnight
in sweet water and stewing since dawn
with tomato and onion, it'll become breakfast.
A thin son of Ba-'Ali leaving the back room
sulks through the shop, greeting no one.

After sunset, he'll head down to the waterfront,
to the teashop where young men play chess,
swatting their timers fiercely after each move.
Two days of traveling away, my wife
takes care of our newborn twins at home.

Bearing my glaringly foreign surname,
they cling to life despite odds impossible
had I not believed in higher hands.
Yet I flew away from them, away from my wife,
away from this republic in search of something else.

But in al-Hudaydah, the sand whipped around fighter planes
junked behind the runway. Over the mountains,
I was jostled from air pocket to pocket like a nervous coin.
At Aden airport, an Egyptian teacher perched on his luggage
for the long layover could only curse. *They are dogs,*

all of them, he said, cigarette smoke knifing out
between his teeth. It was then I knew I had to stay.
I walked out of the airport and called my nearest friend,
a son of Ba-'Ali. A crammed taxi across the desert
for a day, and I arrived. The oldest son of Ba-'Ali

opens the safe, shows me a tray. It's his mother's gold.
His father's eye squints tighter around the jeweler's eyeglass.
When we were introduced, each son shook my hand
and kissed his father's ring. I imagine Ba-'Ali's bride
slipping her fingers into a glove of handcrafted gold mail

and thick coins the first time, the weight a promise asks.
Now I am holding her private gold! On another tray,
old trinkets wait to be melted down and reborn
as whatever is the current rage in Bahrain.
There, I find something to resurrect, something

to grace my wife: big crescent earrings with bangles
dangling in the wane. A son of Ba-'Ali bathes my choice
in solvent until it glows. Soon, I will return home
with bright Indian shawls and gold. When I give her the gold,
she will thank me politely and put it away, forever.

THE OFFICE OF DR. ISHAQ, PEDIATRICIAN

for Fathia

We walk in the open door, past the waiting room
where men, smoking, watch the only channel
on the television perched high on the wall,

into the back hallway, where the receptionist
thumbs through a box of index cards before darting inside a door.
In each corner of the hall, a mother clutches a bundle

of coughs tight as pearls. Our son bears his fever with reserve.
Reappearing from an inside chamber, the receptionist
motions mother and baby in. I wait with the other fathers

because I trust their lead, or perhaps there is another reason
that eludes me now. The singer on the television
is playing an *'oud*, the long stylus differentiating strings

like the leg of a tropical spider. In the examination room,
the doctor weighs our swaddled son on a metal scale.
Not used to breathing smoke, I step outside, where the evening air

settles the dust the city ground today from stone.
A garden nearby perfumes the night with lemongrass,
jasmine, and onion. I know he'll be healed.

RAINY SEASON

I try not to look foolish. But sometimes,
when I'm trundling the big key in the wooden lock,
a chameleon twitches in between the hinges.
Once, it skittered across the ceiling,
fleeing into the folds of the distant bedroom
where our premature twins slept under a gauze tent.
I spent the night watching pockets of air
empty and fill inside their chests.

Babies born in the eighth month never survive,
old women told my wife. But ours
have now crawled to the back door,
where they are clucking their tongues,
coaxing stray cats over walls crowned with broken glass.
The cats sit just out of reach, in tall weeds,
waiting for our daily chicken-intestine charity.
I thank Allah for intestines and tongues.

The only healthy tree in the garden is a sour
pomegranate, whose scarlet coronets blat and blare.
Several months from now, the retired judge
living upstairs will bid me present the fruit
from the highest branches to him. I'll teeter
to reach each gorgeous blushing orb, yank,
but the jeweled chambers will have been gutted
by churlish birds. Still, I'll deliver the skins.

In a few hours, brown torrents will flood the city again.
The market will be cleansed of people, date stones,
egg shells and feathers, banana peels, goat hooves,
all washed into an alluvial plain. As I see it, rain
is a solvent. That's how weeds in empty lots

grow inches overnight, why I spend so much time
in my window the morning before today's rain,
the morning after yesterday's.

PRAYING BESIDE A *MUJAHED*

He and his Kalashnikov have known
more reasons to pray than the *imam* leading us,
who grinds out the same verses as if Allah
were a big deaf ear.

His flak jacket smells of terraced mountains
before the rain, farms of wind rumbling past
as he leans over the cab of a pickup plummeting
into the world's last valley.

After surveying the dead, the brothers
who died with peaceful smiles, he buried them
in gardens of rubble. Soon, red blossoms unfolded
with the promise of musk.

Were I to turn my head to the left, I could gaze
deep into the dark eye of the Kalashnikov.
Never think that a trigger tripped, a skull separated
onto plush carpet, is an accident, for destiny

allows no accidents. After the prayer, we'll say *peace*.
His hand will shake mine with vigor. Until then,
closing my eyes, all I can see are onions, glorious
and sweet, thundering in the damp loam of Heaven.

GLOSSARY OF ARABIC WORDS

'ammi: "my uncle"

'aqeeq: agate

'asr: mid-afternoon; one of the five daily Islamic prayer times

'atoora: perfume

bakhsheesh: tip or small bribe

baqdoonis: parsley

bayt: house

dhow: a traditional one-sailed Arabian ship

diwan: a sitting room, often with cushions lining the walls

duqq: a variety of spiced Yemeni coffee

fajr: pre-dawn; one of the five daily Islamic prayer times

hijrah: literally, "migration," especially the migration of the Prophet Muhammad from Mecca to Medina, the event that marked the start of the Hijri calendar

imam: the prayer leader

insha'Allah: "if Allah wills," a phrase used whenever one speaks about the future

jinn (singular *jinni*)*:* in Islamic cosmology, invisible creatures unhampered by space and time, which some Muslims believe can possess the bodies of humans

kaafir: a non-believer in Islam

mooria: traditional necklace of golden beads worn by married women

muezzin: the person who delivers the prayer call

mujahed: literally, "one who struggles or strives," specifically, those who fought the Soviet forces in Afghanistan in the 1980s

na'na': mint

'oud: Arabian lute

qat: a mildly narcotic plant cultivated in the Red Sea region and chewed socially

qahwa al-Baidhani: a variety of Yemeni coffee brewed in the region of al-Baidha

qishr: a variety of Yemeni coffee made from coffee bean husks

Qur'an: the Islamic holy book

rayhan: basil

rial: Yemeni currency

samsara: a warehouse for grains and goods

sharshaf: black outfit and veil worn by many Yemeni women

sitara: large multicolored cloth worn by women in Old Sana'a

souq: market

Souq al-Nisa': "Women's Market," region of the market where women's clothing and accessories are sold

surah: a chapter of the *Qur'an*

Surat Yaseen: the name of a particular *surah*, which, because it discusses the Hereafter, is sometimes recited in conjunction with funerals

tabbouleh: Levantine salad made from parsley, bulgur, cucumbers, and tomatoes

ABOUT THE AUTHOR

YAHYA FREDERICKSON teaches writing and literature at
Minnesota State University Moorhead. He holds an MFA in
Creative Writing from the University of Montana and a PhD
in English from the University of North Dakota. Between
graduate degrees he taught in Yemen, initially as a Peace
Corps Volunteer. He served as a Fulbright Scholar in Syria in
2005 and in Saudi Arabia in 2011.He is the author of three
chapbooks, including *Month of Honey, Month of Missiles* (Three
by Three: Tigertail Annual, 2009); *Returning to Water* (Dacotah
Territory, 2006); and *Trilogy* (Dacotah Territory, 1985, with
Julie Taylor and Richard Schetnan). His poetry has appeared
in *Arts & Letters, Black Warrior Review, Clackamas Literary Review,
Crab Orchard Review, CutBank, Hanging Loose, Prairie Schooner, The
Southern Review,* and many other journals.